HELICOPTERS

by Darlene R. Stille

Content Adviser: Kathy Bratton, Director of Education and Marketing,
American Helicopter Museum and Education Center,
West Chester, Pennsylvania

Reading Adviser: Dr. Linda D. Labbo,
Department of Reading Education, College of Education,
The University of Georgia

Compass Point Books
Minneapolis, Minnesota

Compass Point Books
3109 West 50th Street, #115
Minneapolis, MN 55410

Visit Compass Point Books on the Internet at *www.compasspointbooks.com* or e-mail your request to *custserv@compasspointbooks.com*

Photographs ©: Morton Beebe/Corbis, cover; Courtesy of Robinson Helicopter Company, 1, 14; Photo Network/Mark Sherman, 4; Photo Network/Nancy Hoyt Belcher, 6; Bettmann/Corbis, 8; Unicorn Stock Photos/Eric R. Berndt, 10–11; Richard Zellner/Sikorsky Aircraft Corp., 12, 18, 22, 24; Richard Hamilton Smith/Corbis, 16; Philip Wallick/Corbis, 20–21; Photo Network/Terry Brandt, 26.

Editor: Christianne C. Jones
Photo Researcher: Svetlana Zhurkina
Designers: Melissa Kes/Jaime Martens

Library of Congress Cataloging-in-Publication Data
Stille, Darlene R.
  Helicopters / by Darlene R. Stille.
         p. cm. — (Transportation)
Includes index.
Summary: A simple introduction to different kinds of helicopters and their uses.
  ISBN 0-7565-0606-9 (hardcover)
  1. Helicopters—Juvenile literature. [1. Helicopters.] I. Title. II. Series.
  TL716.2.S75 2004
  629.133'352—dc22   2003012302

Table of Contents

NOTE: In this book, words that are defined in the glossary
are in **bold** the first time they appear in the text.

What's That Noise?

Listen! Chop, chop, chop! That loud noise means a helicopter is near. Helicopters are sometimes called choppers or copters.

Look! The helicopter goes straight up. The helicopter comes straight down. It flies forward. It flies backward. It can even fly sideways! Helicopters can go in circles or stay in one place.

Feel! The helicopter is landing. The spinning **blades** create a lot of wind. Everything gets blown around.

rotor

blade

tail

tail rotor

How Does It Do That?

A helicopter does not have wings like an airplane. Instead, it has blades on top. The **engine** makes the blades spin. The spinning motion makes the helicopter fly.

The blades are part of the **rotor**. Some big helicopters even have two rotors on top!

The back part of the helicopter is the tail or tail bloom. Some helicopters have a second small rotor on the tail.

The First Helicopters

More than 2,000 years ago, people in China had toy helicopters called flying tops. The blades on the flying tops were made of wood. People only dreamed about flying real helicopters.

Some of the first helicopters were made in France. One of these helicopters had four rotors. Igor Sikorsky, a Russian man who lived in the United States, invented the first helicopter with one main rotor. He flew his chopper in 1939.

 Igor Sikorsky flying a helicopter about 1940

skids

Riding in a Tiny Chopper

Let's take a ride in a small helicopter. It looks like a glass bubble. This helicopter does not have wheels. It sits on two long **skids**. It has two seats. One seat is for you. The other seat is for the pilot.

The pilot uses a **lever**, pedals, and a joystick to make the helicopter go forward, backward, and sideways.

Riding in a Big Chopper

Now, let's take a ride in a big helicopter. This chopper rolls on wheels. You climb up stairs to board the chopper. There are a lot of seats inside. There are also a lot of windows.

The big helicopter has a pilot and a co-pilot. They use pedals, levers, buttons, and switches to fly this helicopter. They also use computers to help them fly.

Flying for Fun

You can take a ride in a helicopter just for fun! You can ride over the Grand Canyon in Arizona. You can take a trip to see big fields of ice called glaciers in Alaska. You can fly close to volcanoes in Hawaii.

You can even take a helicopter to go skiing. The helicopter takes you high up on a mountain. When it is safe, you jump out and ski down.

Choppers at Work

Helicopters can fly almost anywhere. They do many different jobs.

Some choppers spray farm fields to kill bugs that hurt crops. Others carry big machines to the top of tall buildings.

Some choppers take workers and firefighters to high mountains and other places that are hard to get to. Other helicopters are used to rescue people who are in danger.

The Traffic Copter

A traffic copter flies over highways around cities. A police officer or a reporter flies in the helicopter. Any traffic or road problems are reported over the radio.

You hear a radio report from the traffic copter. There is a big crash on the highway. All the cars are stopped. Thanks to the traffic copter, you know you have to take a different road to get home.

Choppers That Fight Fires

A big forest fire is blazing. Firefighters cannot get to the fire with a fire truck. How will the firefighters get to the fire?

A special helicopter can help. The special chopper takes firefighters to the fire. The helicopter drops water on trees and bushes to help put the fire out.

21

Choppers to the Rescue

Choppers can go almost anywhere to help save lives. Choppers can save people trapped by floods or earthquakes.

A boat just sank in the ocean. No other boats are nearby. The passenger is stranded in the water.

Here comes the Coast Guard helicopter to help. A rescue team on the chopper lowers a rope. The passenger is lifted into the chopper. The chopper takes the passenger safely back to shore.

Choppers at War

Helicopters are used in the **military**. The Army, Navy, and Marines all use helicopters.

Some helicopters bring soldiers to battle. Other helicopters carry soldiers or sailors who are hurt to hospitals.

Big helicopters move cannons and small trucks. Other helicopters fire guns and **missiles** during battle.

The Newest Helicopters

The V/STOL is a vertical and short takeoff and landing aircraft. It has wings and engines to make it fly fast like a plane. It can go straight up or down like a helicopter.

The robot helicopter is another new type of helicopter. Is does not need a pilot. Instead, it is computer programmed. A robot helicopter can go to very dangerous places.

The newest helicopters will help people in many ways.

◀ The new V/STOL aircraft

Glossary

blades—the arms of a rotating machine

engine—a machine that changes energy into a force that causes motion

lever—the part of a machine that is like a handle and is pushed or pulled to operate the machine

military—related to the army and other armed forces

missiles—weapons made to be launched through the air toward a target

rotor—rotating part of a machine

skids—long, narrow pieces on the landing gear of certain aircraft

Did You Know?

* The president of the United States uses a helicopter to make short trips.

* Two inventors in France built the first real helicopters. They flew them in 1907. The first helicopters did not fly very well.

* More than 3 million people have been saved by helicopters since 1944.

* Some helicopters are flying ambulances. They have stretchers inside to carry sick or injured people to the hospital.

* Police use helicopters to help catch people who may have committed a crime. Police helicopters have bright lights. The lights help the police search when it is dark outside.

Want to Know More?

At the Library

Bledsoe, Glenn, and Karen Bledsoe. *The World's Fastest Helicopters.* Mankato, Minn.: Capstone Press, 2002.

Englart, Mindi Rose. *Helicopters: From Start to Finish.* San Diego, Calif.: Blackbirch Press, 2002.

Olien, Becky. *Rescue Helicopters.* Mankato, Minn.: Bridgestone Books, 2001.

Richardson, Adele D. *Transport Helicopters.* Mankato, Minn.: Bridgestone Books, 2001.

On the Web

For more information on helicopters, use FactHound to track down Web sites related to this book.

1. Go to *www.compasspointbooks. com/facthound*
2. Type in this book ID: 0756506069
3. Click on the *Fetch It* button.

Your trusty FactHound will fetch the best Web sites for you!

Through the Mail

Smithsonian National Air and Space Museum

7th and Independence Ave. S.W.

Washington, DC 20560

Write to learn more about the history of flying

On the Road

American Helicopter Museum and Education Center

1220 American Blvd.

West Chester, PA 19380

See 40 helicopters on exhibit and take a ride in a helicopter

Index

About the Author

Darlene R. Stille is a science editor and writer. She has lived in Chicago, Illinois, all her life. When she was in high school, she fell in love with science. While attending the University of Illinois, she discovered that she also enjoyed writing. Today she feels fortunate to have a career that allows her to pursue both her interests. Darlene R. Stille has written more than 60 books for young people.